10/03

Dot to Dot
IN THE Sky

Also available in this series:

Dot to Dot in the Sky: Stories in the Stars

Dot to Dot
IN THE Sky

STORIES OF THE PLANETS

Joan Marie Galat

illustrations by
Lorna Bennett

whitecap

For additional information, please contact Whitecap Books Ltd., 351 Lynn Avenue, North Vancouver, British Columbia, Canada V7J 2C4.

Edited by Elizabeth McLean
Cover design by Roberta Batchelor
Interior design by Warren Clark

Printed and bound in Hong Kong

National Library of Canada Cataloguing in Publication Data

Galat, Joan Marie, 1963–
     Dot to dot in the sky : stories of the planets / Joan Marie Galat ; Lorna Bennett, illustrator.

     Includes index.
     ISBN 1-55285-392-6

     1. Planets—Mythology—Juvenile literature. 2. Astronomy—Juvenile literature. I. Bennett, Lorna, 1960– I. Title.
QB602.G34 2002   j523.4   C2002-911397-0

The publisher acknowledges the support of the Canada Council for the Arts and the Cultural Services Branch of the Government of British Columbia for our publishing program. We acknowledge the financial support of the Government of Canada through the Book Publishing Industry Development Program for our publishing activities.

For Mom and Dad,
who have given me
a lifetime of encouragement.
J.M.G.

To the wonderful schoolteachers
who gave me the best that was in their hearts,
making the world of difference in my life:
Elizabeth Ann Sinden, Charmain Allen,
Judy Soper, Jim Deptuck,
and Robin Carson.

L. B.

Acknowledgments

I would like to recognize the assistance given
by Douglas Hube, professor emeritus at the
University of Alberta and former national president (1994–96)
of the Royal Astronomical Society of Canada,
and Elizabeth McLean, thorough and proficient editor
of the *Dot to Dot in the Sky* series.

Contents

You gaze up at the night sky and see a multitude of sparkling dots of light. You know everything you see isn't a star—but where do you begin a search for the planets? It only takes a bit of practice to be able to tell the difference between the planets and the stars, and to read the sky like a map. Soon you will be able to find your way, dot to dot in the sky ... to our closest neighbors, the planets.

The nine planets revolving around our Sun belong to the solar system. Mercury, the closest planet to the Sun, and Venus, next to it, are called inferior planets. Beyond Earth are the superior planets: Mars, then Jupiter, Saturn, Uranus, Neptune, and finally Pluto. The path the planets follow is called an orbit, and they are held in their orbits by the Sun's gravity.

Heavenly bodies have been observed since the first people walked the Earth. Our ancient ancestors identified the five planets nearest to our own, which are all visible with the naked eye. Uranus, Neptune, and Pluto were discovered later with the use of telescopes.

Planets look a lot like stars, but some planets appear more brilliant because they are closer to us. Have you ever noticed a bright object in the night sky that was not twinkling? You may have spotted a planet. Planets shine by reflecting light from the Sun, so their glow does not twinkle as much as starlight.

If you compare a planet's location from night to night, you will be able to follow its movement against the backdrop of stars. "Planet" is derived from a Greek word meaning wanderer. The planets appear to wander because their positions are always changing. They are so much closer to us than the stars, we can see their apparent movement over time. The motion of the stars is not noticeable to the unaided eye—even over many centuries.

If you watch a planet over the course of several months, its apparent motion relative to the stars may seem to go in one direction, slow, stop, and then go the other way. This is because Earth sometimes catches up and passes the planets that move in larger orbits. The farther away a planet is, the more slowly it seems to move through the sky. In contrast, the inner planets, Mercury and Venus, can catch up and pass Earth.

Even though each planet follows an oval path around the Sun, planets may look as if they are moving along a crooked path through the stars. This is because we see the planets from another moving planet—Earth—as we travel in our own orbit.

Like the Sun and Moon, planets rise in the east and set in the west. When planets are high in the sky, you can see them from cities almost as well as from the darker countryside. When planets are near the horizon, pollution and the Earth's atmosphere create more distortion.

THE ZODIAC

Constellations are recognized patterns of stars that form imaginary pictures. All the planets except Pluto are always found in or near the 12 constellations of the zodiac, which form a "highway" in the sky where the Sun, Moon, and planets appear to travel.

The zodiac constellations are:

Aries	the Ram
Taurus	the Bull
Gemini	the Twins
Cancer	the Crab
Leo	the Lion
Virgo	the Virgin
Libra	the Scales
Scorpio	the Scorpion
Sagittarius	the Archer
Capricorn	the Sea Goat
Aquarius	the Water Carrier
Pisces	the Fish

Equipment: Binoculars and Telescopes

If you are not sure whether you are seeing a planet or a star, look through binoculars or a telescope. Depending on the strength of your lens, you may be able to make out the shape of a planet. Except when very close to the horizon, the image of a planet through a telescope will be very steady, whereas a star will "twinkle." Because of its great distance, a star viewed through a small telescope will not look much different than it appears to the unaided eye. It will only appear brighter.

Binoculars are ideal for beginners because they are inexpensive, easier to use, and show a wider view. It is not uncommon for experienced astronomers to use binoculars as well as telescopes.

Binoculars are marked with magnification and lens diameter. A pair of binoculars that is 8x40 magnifies eight times, using a 40-millimetre (1.6-inch) lens. Avoid using binoculars higher than 10-power because they are too heavy to hold for long without shaking.

A good-quality telescope will show even more features, such as the rings around Saturn. Shop carefully for a telescope and make your purchase from a specialist dealer. Good optics, a solid mounting, and a steady tripod are more critical than the power. A 75-mm (3-inch) refractor telescope or a 100-mm (4-inch) reflector telescope will work well for a beginner.

Gods and Mortals

Ancient stargazers looked up at almost the same night sky we see today. Studying the heavens helped them make sense of the world. Following the motion of celestial objects enabled early astronomers to learn about the weather, the changing seasons, and the rise and fall of tides.

Observations of the wandering planets also inspired them to make up stories about their gods, to explain things they did not understand. With each planet representing a different god, the mysterious sky was a natural place for myths and legends to occur.

The early Greeks told many stories about their gods. After conquering the Greeks, the Romans accepted the Greek myths as their own, but changed the gods' names. Today we still call all the planets, except Earth and Uranus, by the names of the Roman gods.

The adventures of the gods were used to explain the mysteries of ancient life. When people had good luck, they believed the gods were granting them favors. If there were terrible storms or earthquakes, people thought the gods were angry. Myths also described where mortals went after death.

Ancient people repeated the myths to teach moral lessons and provide entertainment. The stories were retold so often that details changed before they were written down. Today there are many versions of the myths, but most show gods who were generous one moment and selfish the next.

Gods ruled different aspects of the universe. Some symbolized emotions, such as Aphrodite, the goddess of love. Others stood for nature, such as Poseidon, the god of the sea.

Most of the important gods and goddesses were said to live in northern Greece, on a mountain called Olympus. There was always good music, plenty of food to eat, and nectar to drink. It never rained or snowed on Mount Olympus and the wind never blew too strongly.

Mount Olympus was so high, it was impossible for mortals to climb. They had to wait for the gods to come down from the mountain. Many gods liked to travel to Earth and have adventures with the people, but sometimes they did not want anyone to know they were gods. They disguised themselves by taking the form of animals or people.

Roman names	Greek n
Mercury	Hermes
Venus	Aphrodite
Terra (Earth)	Gaia
Mars	Ares
Jupiter or Jove	Zeus
Saturn	Cronus
Coelus	Uranus
Neptune	Poseidon
Pluto	Hades

The gods acted a lot like humans, but were taller and more handsome or beautiful. They were also more intelligent, with greater wisdom. Gods could not be killed because ichor, which gave them eternal life, flowed inside their bodies instead of blood.

Even kind and generous gods were not perfect, however. They made mistakes, lost their tempers, and reacted with such jealousy that mortals who challenged the gods could expect revenge.

Tales of the unpredictable gods still intrigue people today. Their adventures may reflect our experience of the world back to us. We see that people have always tried to find ways to explain events and make sense of life and death.

THE GREEK CONNECTION

- Mount Olympus really exists. It is the highest mountain in Greece, rising 2917 metres (9570 feet) high.

- The Olympic Games, named for the town of Olympia and created to honor Zeus, were first held in 776 B.C. Every four years, Greek men competed to show their strength and endurance. The winners of the different athletic contests were greatly respected and admired. The modern Olympic Games, which began in 1896, are based on the ancient Greek games.

- Other Greek places featured in myths include Mount Parnassus, which the god Apollo was said to visit often. The city of Athens was named for the goddess Athena, who was thought to protect the people there. Most of the ancient Greek cities were associated with a favorite god, and citizens built temples and held festivals in their god's honor.

The planet Mercury has been known at least since the third millennium B.C. It may have been named Mercury because it travels so quickly across the sky, like the Greek god Hermes—the messenger. The Greeks knew that Mercury was only one planet, but they associated it with two different gods. They called Mercury Apollo when seen as a morning planet and Hermes when spotted at night.

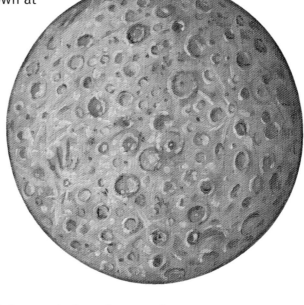

APOLLO
(uh-PAUL-oh)

In a part of Greece called Delphi, sulphur fumes escaped from Mount Parnassus. When a priestess on the mountain sniffed the air and breathed in the sulphur, the potent fumes made her fall into an eternal sleep.

As the priestess slumbered, Mother Earth whispered many secrets. The priestess could hear the murmured secrets in her dreams and repeated them out loud. The prophecies were about the future and always came true. Priests called her the Oracle of Delphi and traveled long distances to hear her words.

The Oracle of Delphi was guarded by a black and scaly dragon called Python. The old dragon was so mean that the birds on the mountain were afraid to sing. He even scared away the nymphs—beautiful maidens who remained eternally young.

The nymphs did not know that Python would not live on the mountain forever, but the dragon knew. The Oracle had warned Python he would be killed by Apollo, the son of Zeus.

Apollo was handsome and popular — loved more than any of the other gods. He had grown very quickly after he was born because he was fed nectar and ambrosia. Apollo was still a youth when Zeus, the supreme ruler of all the gods, called him to come to Mount Olympus. He had special gifts for Apollo, made by Hephaestus, the blacksmith god. Zeus gave Apollo a gold bow with a quiver of golden arrows, as well as a golden chariot with white horses to pull it across the sky.

Apollo practiced using the gifts until he felt ready for adventure, then decided it would be exciting to go to Mount Parnassus and hunt for Python. He climbed into his chariot and flew to Delphi, where he scanned the mountain below, trying to spot the dragon. Soon he caught sight of the creature near its cave on a mountainous slope.

Python looked up and saw Apollo flying toward him in the golden chariot. The dragon knew its life was almost over, but it would not give up without a fight. As Apollo swooped closer, Python gave a terrible hiss, spraying a torrent of fire and poison into the air. The young god dodged the flames, then took aim and fired arrow after golden arrow at the angry

OBSERVING MERCURY

- If you look at Mercury through a small telescope, you can see that it has phases like the Moon. You will usually see it appear between its crescent and its half phases.

- Mercury is only visible for two weeks at a time, a few times a year, making it hard for astronomers to study.

- Look for Mercury low in the eastern sky just before sunrise, or very low in the west just after sunset. Because Mercury is so close to the Sun, it can only be seen near the horizon at dusk or dawn.

- Do not scan for Mercury with binoculars or a telescope when any portion of the Sun is visible. Be very careful not to look at the Sun because you can damage your eyes.

- Mercury appears to twinkle more than the other planets. This is because it is so low in the horizon, we see more distortion when looking through Earth's atmosphere.

dragon. A thousand arrows later, Python lay down its head and died.

Now that the dragon was gone, the nymphs returned to Mount Parnassus, the birds began to sing again, and Apollo sang too.

To celebrate killing the dragon, Apollo started the Pythian Games in ancient Greece. Every four years the winners in foot races, chariot races, and feats of strength were crowned with wreaths of laurel leaves.

Apollo was known as the god of music, archery, light, youth, beauty, poetry, prophecy, agriculture, cattle, and health.

HERMES
(HUR-meez)

Hermes was born as the Sun came up, and he was ready to start the day. This god did not start out as a helpless infant. Instead, his mind developed so quickly he was able to cause trouble his very first day of life. It started when Hermes climbed out of his cradle as his mother lay sleeping. Taking careful steps, he tiptoed past her bed, stepped outside, and wandered over to a nearby field. Hermes saw a fine-looking herd of cows grazing on the grass and clover and began to wish the cattle belonged to him.

The young god decided to steal some of the cows, even though he realized they belonged to his older brother Apollo. He already had a plan to fool Apollo if he tried to find the missing animals.

First, Hermes separated 50 of the finest cows from the rest of the herd. He caught each animal and tied tree bark onto its hooves so that Apollo would not be able to recognize the prints. Hermes wanted to be absolutely sure he would not get caught, so he also tied brooms on each cow's tail to sweep away some of the tracks. When the cows were ready, he tied piles of branches to his own feet too.

The branches made his footprints huge. Hermes led the cows backwards out of the field, so that it looked as if a giant had walked into the field and was still there!

He led the 50 stolen cows into a patch of trees, killed two of them and made strings from their intestines. He attached the strings to a turtle shell and named the instrument a lyre. When the lyre was done, Hermes went back to his cradle and pretended to be asleep.

As Hermes lay in the cradle with his eyes closed, Apollo returned to the field and counted the cows. When he discovered that 50 were missing, he searched everywhere, but could not find his cattle.

Apollo marched up to Hermes' cradle and accused him of stealing the cows. At first Hermes denied it, but Apollo did not believe him and chased the baby all the way to Mount Olympus. Apollo told their father what Hermes had done, insisting that Zeus make Hermes return the cows.

The other gods laughed because Apollo had been tricked by a baby. Zeus wanted to laugh, but did not let Hermes see him smile. He wanted his sons to be friends and made Hermes return the animals, but when Apollo counted the cows, two were still missing.

Apollo became angry again, but Hermes could be very charming. When he showed his brother the lyre he had made out of the turtle shell, Apollo immediately wanted the musical instrument for himself. He offered Hermes the rest of the cows in exchange for the lyre and they made a deal. Zeus was happy to see them become friends.

Zeus told Hermes he should not steal or lie. Hermes said he would try to be better behaved, if Zeus would give him a throne on Olympus. Zeus agreed, also giving him a pair of winged sandals, a golden hat with wings, and a cape to hide his magic wand.

Hermes became the winged messenger of the gods and also guided the souls of the dead to Hades. Hermes was known as the god of travelers, thieves, herds, shepherds, merchants, and luck.

Planetary Notes

- Mercury is the second smallest planet. Its diameter is 4880 km (3032 miles), less than half the size of Earth.

- If you could stand on Mercury and look up, away from the Sun, the sky would look black even in the daytime because there is so little atmosphere.

- After Venus, Mercury is the second slowest spinner. Mercury spins so slowly that it gets very hot in the day and very cold at night. Daytime temperatures can reach 350°C (662°F), with nighttime temperatures dropping to –170°C (–274°F).

- The surface of Mercury is covered with impact craters, caused by comets and chunks of rock (meteorites and asteroids) that slammed onto its surface.

- Mercury and Venus are the only planets that do not have moons.

APHRODITE
(a-fro-DYE-tee)

Normally, as waves crash against each other in the ocean, little pockets of air are trapped as bubbles that burst and disappear. But one day, near the coast of the island of Cythera, the waves started forming more and more bubbles. The bubbles would not pop, and more and more foam floated to the top of the water. The foam rose higher and higher until a silhouette began to develop into the shape of a maiden. Her eyes sparkled, her face shone, and her long flaxen hair was decorated with roses. Aphrodite was so beautiful the wind almost lost its breath.

Aphrodite stepped out of the foamy water and floated across the waves toward land. She stepped ashore and flowers sprang up wherever her feet touched the earth. She was met by three of Zeus's daughters, known as the three Graces. They took her to a conch shell that was pushed up against the beach. Aphrodite climbed into the shell and Zephyr, the god of the west wind, blew the shell to the island of Cyprus. Zeus sent his attendants to meet her and they showed her the way to Mount Olympus, in northern Greece.

The gods on Mount Olympus were so enchanted by Aphrodite's beauty that they offered her a golden throne and named her the goddess of love and beauty.

All the gods adored Aphrodite and tried to impress her with their talents. Poseidon claimed that since she rose from the water, she belonged to him, the god of the sea. To demonstrate his power he pointed his trident toward the

OBSERVING VENUS

- Venus is easy to spot because it is usually brighter than any other planet or star.

- Under favorable circumstances, Venus can be viewed up to three or four hours before dawn or after sunset. It is never visible for the whole night because of its nearness to the Sun. Sometimes Venus can be seen in the daytime.

- Venus can be seen for about one season in the evening sky, and another in the morning sky. The months of visibility change from year to year.

- When Venus travels away from Earth, it is the last object to disappear from the sky in the morning. When Venus is traveling toward Earth, it is the first object visible in the western sky

before sunset. Early astronomers called it both the morning and the evening star, thinking it was two different stars. Venus was known as Hesperus when viewed as the morning "star," and Phosphorus when seen as the evening "star."

- If you look through a small telescope, you will find Venus's phases easier to see than Mercury's.

sea, causing a tidal wave to devastate the shore. Hermes, the messenger god, tried to win her with the promise that they would travel together in his chariot to see the beautiful places of the world. Apollo, the god of music, sang her a love song.

Aphrodite was not ready to choose any of the gods for a husband, for she knew that with her beauty she could have anyone she wanted at any time. But she was not permitted to wait. Hera became so worried when she saw her husband Zeus look lovingly at Aphrodite, she demanded the goddess be married to her son, Hephaestus.

Hephaestus was the god of blacksmiths, craftsmen, and fire. He had been lame since birth and was not handsome, but was hardworking, kind, and very strong. Even though Hephaestus was willing to marry Aphrodite, everyone expected her to refuse.

Much to everyone's surprise, Aphrodite did not argue. She knew Hephaestus would not try to control her as much as the other gods, and this would leave her free to follow her whims.

In his workshop beneath a volcano in Sicily, Hephaestus made his bride a present—a golden girdle, or belt, woven with magic. He did not realize that when Aphrodite wore it, the other gods would fall in love with her even more easily.

Aphrodite eventually showed a preference for her husband's brother, Ares. The other gods did not like Ares much because he was vain and liked to fight too often, but Aphrodite was attracted to his good looks.

One of the things Aphrodite liked to do was help others with their love problems. Her son Cupid was known as love's messenger. He carried a special bow and a quiver full of golden arrows. When Aphrodite wanted someone to fall in love, Cupid

hit the person with an arrow that made gods and mortals fall in love with the next person they saw. Cupid thought it was a lot of fun to shoot people with his arrows and watch what happened.

As well as being called the goddess of love and beauty, Aphrodite is also the goddess of sailors and nature. Sailors prayed to her to calm the wind and the waves because she came from the sea.

Planetary Notes

- Venus and Earth are so close in size they are often called twins.

- Sometimes Venus's light is bright enough to cast shadows. It receives about twice as much sunlight as Earth. Venus looks bright for two reasons: it passes close to Earth and its white clouds reflect 72% of the Sun's light.

- The dense, unbroken layer of clouds that surrounds Venus is made of drops of sulfuric acid, which is strong enough to dissolve metal.

- Venus's atmosphere is 97 km (60 miles) thick, and is composed of carbon dioxide. The carbon dioxide acts like a blanket around the planet, keeping Venus hot because heat cannot escape through its thick atmosphere.

- Even though it is farther from the Sun, Venus is hotter than Mercury. The temperature is greater than 480°C (900°F)— more than four times hotter than boiling water.

- Venus does not have a moon.

- Up to 25 bolts of lightning flash every second on Venus.

GAIA
(GAY-uh)

At the beginning of time, there was only a dark, shapeless emptiness named Chaos. Mother Earth—called Gaia—was born from Chaos. Nobody lived on Earth and Gaia was lonely until she looked up and fell in love with the sky, named Uranus. When it rained, plants, animals, and rivers were formed, making Gaia the mother of life.

Gaia and Uranus had many children. The first three children were born as Cyclops, each with one eye glowing in the middle of its forehead. The Cyclops were known as Brontes, Steropes, and Arges.

Uranus was not pleased with the Cyclops, nor his next children, who were even more monstrous. Each was an incredibly ugly giant with 100 heads. Uranus could not stand to look at the Hundred-Headed

Giants. He reached down, grabbed the frightful young giants and the Cyclops, and hurled them into the deepest, darkest pit he could find under the Earth.

Gaia was angry but there was nothing she could do. Eventually she gave birth to 12 more children, called the Titans, who became known as the first gods. They were so tall, the mountains became their thrones. Uranus and Gaia were very proud of the Titans.

Gaia asked the Titans to set their brothers free, but 11 of the Titans were so afraid of Uranus they refused to help. The youngest Titan, named Cronus, was stronger than the others and used a flint scythe to fight his father. When he wounded Uranus, three drops of blood fell to the earth. The drops transformed into horrible creatures with bat wings, snakes for hair, and black doglike bodies. These strange beasts became known as the Furies of the underworld.

ASTEROIDS AND EARTH

- An asteroid is a chunk of rock or metal in space, usually considered to be greater than a kilometre (0.6 mile) in diameter.

- Astronomers estimate there is a chance of an asteroid hitting Earth once every 300,000 years.

- One theory suggests that dinosaurs became extinct after an asteroid hit Earth. There is a huge crater in Mexico, where a comet or asteroid may have collided with our planet 65 million years ago. Gas and dust from the explosion would have reduced the amount of sunlight reaching Earth for many months, or even years. The gas would have caused acid rain, killing most forms of plant life and, eventually, the dinosaurs that depended on the plants.

- Scientists in different parts of the world watch for asteroids that may come too close to Earth. They expect to know ten to hundreds of years ahead of time if an asteroid might hit us. If they discover that an asteroid's orbit may take it too close to Earth, they will try to either blow it up or deflect it off course.

- Earth's thick atmosphere burns up most of the meteoroids (chunks of rock or metal smaller than asteroids) that come our way.

Planetary Notes

- The Earth travels around the Sun at 107,240 km/hour (66,635 miles/hour).

- Earth is not a perfect sphere. It is slightly flatter at the poles and it bulges at the equator.

- If you wrapped a very long measuring tape around Earth's equator, it would measure 40,076 km (24,903 miles).

- Unlike the other planets, Earth is mostly covered with water. It is the only planet in our solar system that has water on it as a solid, liquid, and gas. Water covers 75% of the Earth.

- Earth is also different because it has oxygen in the atmosphere—in fact, 21% of our atmosphere is oxygen.

- We have seasons because the Earth is tilted on its axis. During summer, your part of the Earth is tilted toward the Sun.

As Uranus lay suffering, he predicted that Cronus would one day endure the same fate and be conquered by his own son.

Cronus became god of the universe. He ruled both Heaven and Earth, but angered Gaia by refusing to let his brothers go. Gaia had no choice but to wait for the grandchild who would be stronger than Cronus.

ARES
(AIR-eez)

Zeus and Hera had a son named Ares. The boy grew up to be tall and handsome, but he also had a raging temper. He loved a battle and got excited whenever he heard someone brawling. Mortals often asked for his help when they wanted to settle a disagreement, for they knew Ares would not care who was right or wrong. He was willing to fight for any cause, and would sometimes fight for no reason at all.

Even though Ares was the god of war, he did not win all his fights and when he lost, he was a sore loser. He cried when he got hurt and ran back to Zeus to be healed. Ares was lucky to be an immortal god because he could fight as much as he wanted without fear of dying.

Ares was such a trouble-maker, no one except Aphrodite liked to be around him. She loved Ares despite his bad moods and brutal temper, and put up with his faults because he was so handsome.

Hades was the only other god who did not mind Ares fighting, for whenever there was a war more dead souls entered the underworld, where Hades ruled.

In one fight, Ares joined Zeus in a battle against two giants, Otus and Ephialtes, sons of Poseidon, the sea god. The two giants had decided to pile two mountains on top of each other, then use the mountains like steps to get to Mount Olympus and overthrow Zeus. But the giants could not rip the mountains off the Earth without being seen. Zeus discovered their plan and called his armies to battle.

Ares fought to protect Mount Olympus, but was taken prisoner by the giants. They stuffed him in a large bronze jar and hid him in a barn. The battle continued without the god of war, finally ending when Zeus overpowered the giants.

With Olympus safe, the other gods began searching for Ares. They looked for a very long time and hunted in many places, but there was no sign of Ares and they finally gave up.

Still trapped in the jar as a

OBSERVING MARS

- Earth catches up to Mars and passes it about every two years and two months. This is the best time to observe this planet.

- The appearance of Mars changes dramatically, depending how close it is to Earth. Sometimes its brightness can be compared to the stars in the Big Dipper. Other times, Mars may appear as luminous as Jupiter.

- Mars looks like a very small red disk when viewed through binoculars.

- The polar ice caps on Mars can be seen with a large telescope. You can see how they have grown and shrunk if you observe them on a regular basis.

- Planet-wide dust storms sometimes occur when Mars reaches its closest point to the Sun. These storms make it hard to see any details on the planet.

helpless prisoner, the god of war became very thin. Ares had no room to move and, without exercise, he lost his strength.

Thirteen months later, Ares was still trapped in the jar. The Sun was setting when at last someone pushed open the door of the barn. It was his half-brother Hermes, often called the god of luck. He was looking for a place to sleep and lay down on a pile of hay. Hermes was almost asleep when a tapping sound made him open his eyes. He thought he was hearing rats, but closed his eyes again and tried to ignore the noise.

When it did not stop, the god sighed and got up. He followed the sound of the tapping to the bronze jar. Curious now, Hermes forgot about being tired and dragged the jar into the moonlight. When he knocked on its side, the tapping became so fast and urgent that Hermes pried the leaden top off the jar.

Filled with relief, Ares limped out of his prison and promised Hermes a reward for freeing him.

Ares was also called the god of fertility and agriculture, but was best known for his interest in war.

Planetary Notes

- The reddish-orange soil of Mars contains rust, or iron oxide. Mars is called the red planet because of the iron oxide dust blowing in its atmosphere.

- More than a billion asteroids form a belt between Mars and Jupiter.

- In 1877, an American astronomer named Asaph Hall was searching for moons around Mars. He was about to give up, but his wife encouraged him to keep looking for just one more night. The very next night he discovered Phobos and Deimos.

- Neither of the moons of Mars has very strong gravity. If you were on Deimos, you could launch yourself into space if you could run 35 km/hour (22 miles/hour). If Phobos orbited a bit closer to Mars, it would break up from the force of the planet's gravity and the pieces would form a ring around Mars.

- The largest volcano on Mars is called Olympus Mons. It is named after Mount Olympus, the mythical home of the Greek gods. The volcano is about 600 km (375 miles) across and rises higher than 26 km (16 miles).

ZEUS
(ZOOS)

Zeus was the king of the gods and the god of the sky. He was also called a weather god and the master of thunder, lightning, rain, and light. Although he was stronger than all the other gods combined, he was a fair ruler. He shared his power with his brothers and sisters, as well as six of his children and Aphrodite, the goddess of love. Zeus divided the universe, keeping the heavens for himself, but giving Poseidon the sea and Hades the underworld. His palace sat atop Mount Olympus, hidden in the clouds over Greece.

Ruling from the highest golden throne, Zeus always kept a pail of thunderbolts nearby. When he lost his temper and reached for a thunderbolt, even the other gods were afraid. Zeus's wife, Hera, once stole a thunderbolt, making him so angry that he tied anvils to her feet and hung her up in the sky. Zeus did not let her go until he was convinced she was truly sorry.

Zeus was also the protector and ruler of all humans. He created people with the help of Prometheus, one of the Titans. Prometheus was the god of fire, as well as a trickster. When he made the first people out of clay, Zeus brought them to life.

At first, the people on Earth lived simple lives because they did not know how to do many things. They did not have fire, and without heat they could not form tools out of metal. They could not bake clay to make dishes and were forced to eat all their food uncooked. The only way they could keep warm was by wearing animal furs.

Zeus did not want the people to learn about fire. He worried that they would become too smart and might try to take over his throne. But Prometheus loved the people he had formed from clay. He trusted them and wanted to make their lives easier by giving them fire. He argued with Zeus, but the ruler of the gods would not change his mind.

Prometheus knew that a fire was always burning at Olympus and quietly made his way to the mountain. He made sure no one saw him as he took a glowing

OBSERVING JUPITER

- Jupiter is the largest planet in our solar system, and the brightest planet after Venus. It shines so brightly because its dense, cloudy atmosphere reflects 45% of the sunlight that reaches it.

- Jupiter's four largest moons can be seen with binoculars or a small telescope. Io, Europa, Ganymede, and Callisto appear in an approximately straight line, in the plane of Jupiter's equator. If you observe Jupiter on different nights, you can see their changing positions.

- The Great Red Spot on Jupiter can be seen with a telescope. This massive storm was first noticed in 1664, some 340 years ago. It is like a hurricane, stretching up to 13 km (8 miles) high, 32,000 km (20,000 miles) wide, and 40,000 km (25,000 miles) long.

piece of coal from the fire, then brought the coal back to Earth.

Prometheus gathered the people around him and lit the first fire on Earth. At first Zeus did not know that Prometheus had disobeyed him, and Prometheus was able to teach the people how to use fire to make their lives more comfortable. They learned how to bake clay to make pots, vases, and bricks, as well as how to cook food, and melt metal to build tools and weapons.

One night Zeus looked down from the sky, saw smoke rising from Earth, and realized that Prometheus had tricked him.

Zeus wanted revenge. He appeared on Earth and chained Prometheus to a mountain. Each day an eagle flew up to the god of fire and pecked at his liver. Every morning his liver grew back and the eagle returned to eat again. Prometheus was stuck on the mountain for many years before being rescued by Zeus's son, Hercules.

Zeus also took out his anger on the people who used fire. He told Hephaestus to make a woman out of clay, who would be called Pandora. The goddesses dressed her in a silver cloak and put flowers in her hair. Zeus made the other gods and goddesses teach Pandora many skills. Aphrodite taught her how to bewitch men, while Athena taught her how to sew and cook. Hermes taught her cunning and deceit.

Finally, Zeus gave Pandora a special copper box and told her to keep it near, but to never lift its lid. Pandora was sent to Earth and offered as a wife to Prometheus's brother, Epimetheus. The box was her dowry—a treasure that she brought to her husband.

Epimetheus understood that the box must not be opened and he locked it away. Pandora was happy in her marriage, but as time went on she could not control her curiosity. Believing that the box was full of jewelry, she asked her husband to let her peek into it, but he refused

- Jupiter is a gas giant, made up of hydrogen, helium, methane, and ammonia. Within the gas is a ball of liquid and an inner core of rocky metal. A rocket could never land on Jupiter because the pressure from the gas would break it apart.

- If you could fill Jupiter, it would hold 1323 Earths. Jupiter's diameter is 11 times larger than Earth's.

- There are now 39 known moons around Jupiter—11 of them were discovered in 2002.

- Jupiter's largest moon, Ganymede is the biggest moon in our solar system. It is even bigger than the second smallest planet, Mercury.

- Jupiter rotates faster than all of the other planets in our solar system. It turns at 45,500 km/hour (28,300 miles/hour).

and kept the key safely on his belt.

Epimetheus was a deep sleeper, so one day Pandora waited until he was snoring and gently removed the key from her husband's belt. She set the copper box on a table and with shaking hands removed the lid. A roar filled her ears as an enormous wind rose out of the box. Pandora tried desperately to close the lid, but it was too late, for the rushing air contained all the troubles of the world. There was no way for Pandora to force the wind back into the box. The worries of the world scattered everywhere, forcing humans to live with poverty, aging, illness, envy, weakness, yearning, suffering, and mistrust.

Now Zeus could be sure that humankind would never be able to rise up against him. But as Pandora frantically fastened the lid of the box, she trapped the only good thing that was in it—hope. Even though all types of suffering had been released into the world, people would be able to endure because hope did not escape and would always be near.

CRONUS
(CROW-nuss)

Cronus was the strongest and most courageous son of Uranus and Gaia (Mother Earth). After defeating Uranus, Cronus became the supreme ruler of the universe. He reigned over his brothers, the Titans, who later became known as the old gods. This period was a happy time called the Golden Age. There was no fighting, no stealing, and no need for laws.

Life might have remained peaceful if Gaia had not been so angry, but she missed her first-born children, the one-eyed Cyclops and the Hundred-Headed Giants. They were trapped inside the Earth and Cronus refused to rescue them.

Gaia realized that her children would not be free until there was a new leader. She remembered Uranus's prophecy that Cronus would one day be overthrown by a more powerful son.

Cronus also thought about his father's words, for he did not want to have a child who would grow up to be stronger than him. Every time his wife Rhea had a baby, Cronus swallowed the child. Angrily, Gaia watched and waited.

Rhea was heartbroken when Cronus swallowed her babies. The next time Rhea was pregnant, she made plans with Gaia to save the baby from Cronus by dressing a stone in baby clothes. Cronus was fooled and swallowed the rock, thinking he had swallowed another infant.

The baby god, called Zeus, was taken away to be raised on an island far away from his father. Gaia helped protect Zeus by getting the sprites to beat their shields with swords whenever he cried. There was so much noise, Cronus could not hear the baby.

Zeus grew up and married his first wife, Metis—the goddess of prudence. Known for giving good advice, she told Zeus not to take the throne from Cronus without powerful help.

Metis realized that the babies Cronus had swallowed must still be alive, for they were immortal gods and could not be killed. She knew they would be willing to fight alongside her husband.

Visiting Cronus, Metis offered him a special herb, telling him that it would protect him from his enemies. Cronus accepted the plant and ate it, but quickly discovered that the herb was magical in a different way than he expected. It made him spit up the rock and the five babies he had swallowed.

OBSERVING SATURN

- Saturn is brighter than most stars. It can be seen with the naked eye, but a small telescope is needed to see its rings.

- When looking at Saturn through binoculars, you will see a disk that appears to have an elongated shape. This is because Saturn's rings appear fuzzy when viewed through binoculars.

- About every 14 years, Saturn's rings are almost impossible to see because their edges are tilted our way.

- Saturn's largest moon, Titan, is bigger than Mercury and is the second largest moon in our solar system. It is the only moon to have an atmosphere, which is made up of nitrogen and methane. You can see Titan with most good amateur telescopes. A 150-mm (6-inch) telescope will allow you to also see three other moons: Rhea, Dione, and Tethys.

Hades, Poseidon, Demeter, Hera, and Hestia were happy to be free. They joined Zeus to fight their father, but the Titans sided with Cronus.

The war between the old and new gods lasted such a long time that Zeus needed more help. He traveled to the underworld to free the Hundred-Headed Giants and the Cyclops, and Gaia was at last reunited with her children.

The Cyclops rewarded Zeus with the gift of the thunderbolt. Poseidon received a three-pronged spear, called a trident, and Hades was given a helmet that made him invisible. They used their gifts in the fight against their father. Hades sneaked into Cronus's chambers and opened the doors for his brothers. Poseidon used the trident to distract Cronus so that Zeus could kill him with a thunderbolt.

The Titans continued to fight, but it was hard without a leader. When the Cyclops tired, Zeus brought in the Hundred-Headed Giants. They threw boulders at the Titans, who finally gave up and ran away.

The Titans were forced to live deep inside Earth, where they still cause trouble by making earthquakes and volcanoes. Atlas was the only Titan allowed to remain above ground, but he was cursed to carry the heavens on his shoulders.

Planetary Notes

- Saturn's three rings are 90 metres (300 feet) thick and 275,000 km (171,000 miles) in diameter. Each ring is made up of ringlets of particles of ice and snow. Some bits of ice are as small as dust, while others are as big as a house.

- Saturn has 18 named moons, and several more in the process of being identified. New moons are sometimes discovered when Saturn's rings appear on edge.

- The second-largest planet, Saturn is 10 times bigger than Earth, with a diameter of 120,000 km (74,500 miles).

- Saturn has a cloudy atmosphere. Like Jupiter, Saturn is mostly made up of hydrogen gas. The outer gassy portion surrounds liquid hydrogen and a solid core. If there was an ocean big enough to hold Saturn, the planet would float.

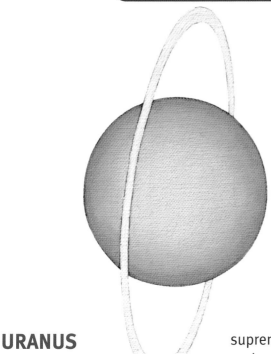

URANUS
(YOOR-uh-nuss)

Uranus was the mate of Mother Earth, or Gaia. At the beginning of time, Uranus grabbed hold of the swirling mass of chaos that made up the world and formed it into the shape we call Earth. Uranus became the earliest supreme god, but for someone so important, little is known about his character. More myths were told about his descendants.

Uranus was defeated by his son Cronus, who became the supreme ruler until he was replaced in turn by his son Zeus. An oracle told Zeus it would be no different for him. His first child would be a daughter, but if there was a second child it would be a son and the next supreme god.

Like his ancestors, Zeus was very afraid of losing his position as leader of the gods. When Metis announced that she was pregnant, Zeus did not wait to see if it would be a boy or girl. He asked his wife to come close to him, then leaning forward, Zeus swallowed Metis.

Now instead of a wife, Zeus had a throbbing headache. No matter what he did, Zeus could not rid himself of the pain. Finally he told Hephaestus, the blacksmith god, that an evil spirit was trapped inside him. Hephaestus took a giant hammer and pounded a wedge into Zeus's skull. Instead of an evil spirit, a young girl stepped out, dressed in armor and carrying a spear. Zeus realized this was his daughter. He was so enchanted with her blue eyes and fair hair that he could not turn her away. Athena became the goddess of arts, crafts, and war, as well as industry, justice, and skill.

One of Athena's skills was spinning wool and weaving cloth into tapestries. Like many gods, she did not want to be bested. When that happened, she could not control her jealousy.

The target of Athena's temper was Arachne, a seventeen-year-old village girl. Arachne was a masterful weaver. The more she practiced her art, the quicker she could work. Her ideas were original and each project was more impressive than the last.

Arachne's latest undertaking was a tapestry portraying the lives of the gods. The characters woven with her thread looked so real, they seemed to move. The other villagers could not stop talking about the beautiful tapestry. Arachne began to feel

OBSERVING URANUS

Uranus looks like a star, and even binoculars will reveal it only as a dot. To be sure you are looking at Uranus and not a star, you will need a planet schedule (see Planet Gazing at the back of this book). A telescope will make the job even easier.

Orbiting Uranus are 22 known moons, but none can be seen with binoculars. An experienced amateur with a very large telescope may be able to locate four of the moons.

so proud of her talent, she bragged that even the goddess Athena could not produce a better tapestry.

Arachne's words were repeated to Athena, who decided she must see the girl's artwork for herself. She went to the village where Arachne lived and asked to see the tapestry. Arachne was honored to be visited by the great goddess, but also a little worried that Athena might have heard about her bragging.

Athena lifted Arachne's tapestry and examined the cloth carefully. She was surprised by the meticulous work of the young village girl. As Athena realized that her own tapestries could never be this enchanting, her curiosity turned to rage. The furious goddess dug her hands into the folds of the tapestry, ripping and tearing the cloth until it was nothing but bits of colored cloth and thread floating to the Earth.

Arachne stepped back from the wild goddess and watched the destruction of her masterpiece. When the last thread touched the ground, the broken-hearted girl turned and walked into the nearby forest.

Looking at the tattered remains of the tapestry, Athena's good humor returned—but she still did not want anyone to be better than her at weaving. She followed Arachne into the woods and turned her into a spider. Now Arachne could still spin beautiful patterns, but never again would anyone think she was a better weaver than Athena.

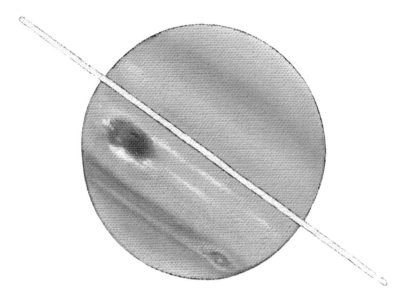

POSEIDON
(puh-SYE-dun)

When Zeus became the supreme ruler, he made his brother Poseidon god of the sea. Poseidon was to be in charge of all the parts of Earth covered with water. At first Poseidon was happy with his huge kingdom and built an underwater castle styled with white turrets and arching doorways. The palace was decorated with coral, shells, and pictures of sea monsters. Poseidon lived in the castle with his queen, the sea goddess Amphitrite.

Poseidon still had the powerful, three-tined trident made by the Cyclops and he controlled the seas with it. When he used the trident to create the first horse from a rock, he also became known as the god of horses. His stunning white chariot horses, with golden manes and hooves, lived in an underwater stable.

But as time went on, the seas, the palace, and the horses were not enough to keep Poseidon happy. The god of the sea felt restless, and became moody and violent. When Poseidon lost his temper, he pointed his trident to split the seas and make mountains burst from the ground. The people blamed Poseidon whenever there was an earthquake, and called him the Earthshaker.

Poseidon decided he wanted authority over the land as well as the sea. He plotted to take over the city of Athens from Zeus's daughter Athena, the goddess of war. The bad-tempered sea god boasted that he could do greater things for the city than Athena. When his niece challenged him to prove what he could do, Poseidon reached for his trident and struck the Earth. A spring flowed from the rock where the prongs touched. At first it seemed like a wonderful gift for the city, but instead of fresh drinking water, only salt water came from the spring.

Athena decided she must also give the city a gift. She planted the first olive tree in Athens and leaves immediately began to grow. Soon the city could enjoy its fruit, oil, and wood. A branch from Athena's olive tree came to mean peace.

OBSERVING NEPTUNE

- Chemicals in Neptune's thick atmosphere contribute to the planet's bluish color.
- Neptune is slightly smaller than Uranus and harder to locate because of its greater distance from the Earth.
- Check a planet visibility schedule (see Planet Gazing at the back of this book) to find out where to begin your search. A telescope is essential to help you determine whether you are looking at a star or at Neptune's disk.

Poseidon sneered at Athena's gift, declaring they must fight to settle who would rule Athens. Athena did not want to lose control of her city and agreed to a battle, but as the stronger god, Poseidon expected to win.

Zeus did not want to see a war between Poseidon and Athena. Before the fight could take place, he gathered together a group of gods and asked them to decide who had given the city the more useful gift. The gods voted for Poseidon, while the goddesses supported Athena, allowing her to win by one vote. Poseidon was so angry, he flooded Athens with towering waves, ruining the temple, as well as houses, farms, and villages. Still, he was forced to give up his plan to rule the city.

Planetary Notes

- The fourth-largest planet in our solar system, Neptune receives only .01% of the sunlight we get on Earth.

- The winds on Neptune are stronger than on any other planet. Wind speeds can reach up to 2000 km/hour (1200 miles/hour).

- Neptune has eight known moons.

- A faint ring system was discovered around Neptune in 1984. The rings contain nonreflective dust particles.

- Astronomers suspected that another planet might exist beyond Uranus, before Neptune was actually discovered. They thought the uneven orbit of Uranus might be caused by the gravity of another planet. Using mathematical formulas, the astronomers figured out what part of the sky to search and discovered the eighth planet!

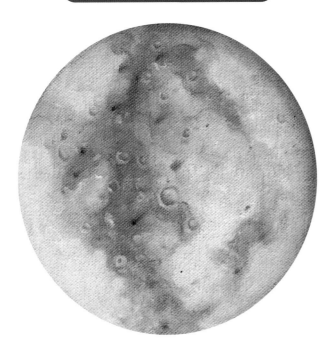

HADES
(HAY-deez)

Hades was the ruler of the underworld, or kingdom of the dead, which was also called Hades. When people died, their souls went to live in Hades whether they had been good or bad.

People could reach the underworld in two ways, either by approaching from the far west or by entering any crevice down into the earth.

Hermes, the messenger god, helped them find their way to the underworld. He brought his travelers to the River Styx, which means hateful or gloomy river. A ferryman named Charon took people across the river in his boat. People were buried with a coin in their mouth so they could pay for the ride, as the unfriendly Charon would not take them if they did not have any money. Those who could not pay were doomed to live on the other side of the river and could come back to haunt the living.

When the dead souls arrived at Hades, they drank from the Pool of Lethe. The water made them forget everything in their previous life.

The underworld was divided into different areas. People who had pleased the gods by being good or brave went to the far west, where their spirits could live in peace. People who had angered the gods suffered in Tartarus, a dark and horrible place.

Once souls came to the underworld, they could not leave, for the gate was locked and the entrance guarded by a three-headed dog named Cerberus.

Hades was a glum and cheerless god, even though he owned all the treasures in the ground. He was a fair ruler of the dead souls, but still the other gods did not like him. He rarely spoke and almost never left his kingdom.

Hades made his judges decide the fate of people coming to the underworld. Rhadamanthys, Minos, and Aeacus were sons of Zeus who had been chosen as judges for their fairness and integrity. They could send the newly arrived souls to everlasting happiness or never-ending torment. Hades would only intervene if the judges disagreed, and his decision was always final.

Hades sometimes wore a

OBSERVING PLUTO

- Pluto is such a dim planet that at least a 30-cm (12-inch) telescope is needed to see it.

- Pluto is the only planet that cannot be seen as a disk when looking through an amateur telescope.

- After you think you have located Pluto, watch it over the next several nights or weeks. Observe its movement through the background of faint stars to be sure it is a "wanderer," not a star.

helmet that made him invisible. Mortals were so afraid of him, they tried not to say his name. They worried that Hades might be nearby and decide to bring them to the underworld if he overheard them.

Sometimes Hades went above ground to chase nymphs, but still he was lonely. He wanted to find a wife.

Zeus decided to help his brother by giving Hades permission to marry Persephone, the beautiful daughter of Demeter, goddess of the harvest. But Persephone did not want to live in the dark underworld and she did not want to leave her mother. Unconcerned with Persephone's wishes, Zeus encouraged Hades to kidnap the bride-to-be.

Hades traveled up into the sunshine in a golden chariot pulled by black horses. He found Persephone walking alone and picking flowers. Grabbing the bewildered girl, Hades forced her into his carriage. They rode back to the dark and dreary underworld, where Hades made Persephone his queen.

Hades sat Persephone on a

Planetary Notes

- Astronomers thought that a ninth planet might exist, but it took 20 years of searching before Pluto was discovered in 1930 by Clyde Tombaugh, in Arizona. The planet was named after a suggestion by an 11-year-old girl— Venitia Burney.

- Pluto has the most elongated orbit of all the planets. From 1979 to 1999, Pluto was closer to Earth, making Neptune the outermost planet. This happens every 248 years.

- Pluto is the solar system's smallest planet. Some astronomers think Pluto should not be classified as a planet. Its size and physical nature make it more like a class of objects beyond Neptune, called trans-Neptunian objects or Kuiper Belt objects.

- Pluto's only moon, Charon, is about half the size of Pluto.

black marble throne. He gave the beautiful queen many precious jewels, but they did not make her happy. He tempted her with delicious fruits, but she refused to eat. Instead, she cried and cried for her mother.

Demeter was devastated when her daughter did not return from her walk. She looked everywhere on Earth for Persephone, and was too upset to take care of the grain growing in the fields. She neglected the Earth until all the plants began to wither. Nothing could grow while the goddess of the harvest was unhappy.

Demeter tried to find someone who might have seen Persephone disappear. She asked the Sun, but its face had been hidden by dark clouds when Persephone vanished. Finally Demeter met a swineherd who could help. He told her he had heard the sound of a girl screaming as the Earth closed up, and Demeter realized that Persephone had been taken by Hades.

She demanded that Zeus bring her daughter back, but the king of the gods refused to help. Demeter became very angry— so angry that she refused to let the Earth be green again. Plants stopped growing in the fields, animals could find nothing to eat, and people began to starve. Zeus was forced to change his mind and told Hades he must let Persephone go.

Even Hades had to listen to Zeus, but before he let her go Hades tricked his queen into eating four pomegranate seeds. Because she had eaten in the kingdom of the dead, Persephone had to stay for part of each year in the underworld—one month for every seed she had eaten. When she was with her mother, good weather came and made the Earth green and full of life. But each fall, when Persephone had to return to the underworld, Demeter became sad again. Winter arrived and everything on Earth died until mother and daughter were reunited in spring.

Planet Facts

	Mercury	Venus	Earth	Mars
Planet Color	White with a tinge of pale yellow, reflecting the Sun's color.	White with a slightly stronger tinge of yellow, a combination of the color of sunlight and Venus's clouds.	Blue and white.	Pale orange-red; observation through a large telescope reveals gray markings that can seem green in contrast to the red background. Mars is the only planet whose color is distinct with the unaided eye or a small telescope.
How Far to the Sun?	58 million km (36 million miles)	108 million km (67 million miles)	150 million km (93 million miles)	228 million km (142 million miles)
How Long Is a Day? A day is the length of time it takes a planet to rotate once on its axis.	59 Earth days	243 Earth days	24 hours	24 hours, 37 minutes
How Long Is a Year? A year is the length of time it takes a planet to orbit the Sun.	88 Earth days	224.7 Earth days	365 Earth days	1.9 Earth years
What Would You Weigh? Some planets have weaker gravity than Earth, while some have stronger gravity. If you weigh 45 kg (100 pounds) on Earth, you will weigh:	17 kg (38 pounds)	41 kg (91 pounds)	45 kg (100 pounds)	17 kg (38 pounds)

Jupiter	Saturn	Uranus	Neptune	Pluto
Very slightly off-white; a mixture of pale yellow, orange, and brown viewed through a large telescope.	Pale yellowish disk with whiter rings.	Pale bluish-green.	Pale blue.	Slightly off-white, reddish-orange tinge.
778 million km (483 million miles)	1.4 billion km (0.9 billion miles)	2.9 billion km (1.8 billion miles)	4.5 billion km (2.8 billion miles)	5.9 billion km (3.7 billion miles)
9 hours, 50 minutes	10 hours, 40 minutes	17 hours, 14 minutes	16 hours, 3 minutes	6.5 Earth days
12 Earth years	29.5 Earth years	84 Earth years	164.8 Earth years	247.7 Earth years
114 kg (252 pounds)	48 kg (106 pounds)	41 kg (90 pounds)	51 kg (113 pounds)	3.6 kg (8 pounds)

Ancient people first observed the heavens to make sense of events on Earth. Early astronomers patiently followed the paths of these planets and recorded their observations. They learned many things about the heavens without any of the technological tools we have today.

Like the first scientists, you can also search the night sky for planets. Whether you use binoculars, a telescope, or just your own eyes, it's fun to observe the paths of the planets, wandering among the backdrop of stars.

Planets are not shown on star maps because their locations are always changing and sometimes they cannot even be seen. To discover the best time to view planets in your part of the world, check current copies of magazines such as *SkyNews, Sky & Telescope, Astronomy,* and the *Observer's Handbook,* published annually by the Royal Astronomical Society of Canada. Some stores sell calendars that show which planets are visible each month in that year. Or you might want to call your nearest Space or Science Centre. Astronomy clubs often produce newsletters. Visit my website at www.joangalat.com to find current astronomy links.

Searching the night sky and making observations can be a rewarding pastime. The space between the other planets and Earth represents mind-boggling distances and vast periods of time. Scientists have been studying the night sky for centuries, yet even now amateur astronomers sometimes make important discoveries.

When you find the planets, remember their namesakes—the great mythical gods of ancient times. The stories of the ancient gods are as fascinating as the planets themselves.

Glossary

acid rain acid precipitation in the form of rain.

ambrosia the food of the Greek and Roman gods.

asteroid a chunk of rock or metal in space, usually considered to be greater than a kilometre (0.6 mile) in diameter. Many asteroids are found between the orbits of Mars and Jupiter.

astronomer a person who studies astronomy.

astronomy the science of studying celestial bodies, including distance, brightness, size, motion, position, and composition.

atmosphere the gases that surround a celestial body such as a planet.

axis an imaginary line through the center of a celestial object, around which the object turns. The line forming the Earth's axis goes through the north and south poles.

celestial relating to the sky.

comet a celestial object of ice, rock, and dust that orbits the Sun. When comets pass near the Sun, they develop a tail of gas and dust that points away from the Sun.

constellation a group of stars that represents an imaginary figure and belongs to one of the 88 officially recognized star patterns, used to define different areas of the sky.

crater a hollow formed by the impact of a meteorite or asteroid.

Cyclops mythical giants with a single eye in the middle of the forehead.

diameter the length of a straight line passing through the center of an object, such as a sphere.

equator an imaginary circle around a planet or moon that divides the north and south hemispheres, halfway between the north and south poles.

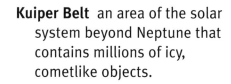

gas giant a large planet that is mostly made up of a very deep, dense gaseous atmosphere.

gravity the force that causes objects to fall or to be pulled toward another object.

ichor the fluid that substituted for blood in ancient Greek gods.

immortal able to live forever.

inferior planet a planet whose orbit lies inside Earth's orbit, that is, Venus and Mercury.

Kuiper Belt an area of the solar system beyond Neptune that contains millions of icy, cometlike objects.

luminous emitting or reflecting light.

meteor a streak of light seen in the sky, caused by fragments of rock and dust burning up as they enter the Earth's atmosphere. Meteors are also called falling stars or shooting stars.

meteorite a meteoroid that hits the surface of a planet or moon.

meteroid a chunk of rock in space, considerably smaller than an asteroid.

moon the natural satellite of a planet. The Earth's satellite is called the Moon, while other planets' moons are given individual names (such as Phobos and Deimos, the two small moons of Mars).

mortal unable to live forever.

myth a story used to explain an event, practice, belief, or natural occurrence.

nectar the drink of the Greek and Roman Gods.

new gods the gods of Mount Olympus.

nymph a beautiful semi-divine woman who lives in mountains, forests, trees, and water.

old gods the giant Titans, who were the first gods to rule the universe.

Olympic Games athletic competitions held every four years, named for the town of Olympia and created to honor Zeus.

Olympus a mountain in Greece where the gods were said to live.

oracle a person through whom a god or goddess speaks.

orbit the path of one celestial body around another.

phases the size of the luminous part of a planet or moon, as seen from Earth.

planet a celestial object of rock or gas that orbits a star. Planets do not produce light, but shine by reflecting the light of a star.

pole the ends of the axis of a sphere.

prophecy the prediction of a future event.

Pythian Games ancient games held at Delphi every four years.

rotate to spin around an axis or center. The Earth rotates once every 24 hours.

solar system a star and the celestial bodies that orbit it. Our solar system includes the Sun, comets, millions of asteroids, more than 60 moons, and the 9 planets.

sprite an elf or fairy.

star a hot sphere of glowing gas that emits energy and light, like our Sun.

superior planet a planet whose orbit lies outside Earth's orbit, that is, Mars, Jupiter, Saturn, Uranus, Neptune, and Pluto.

tide the rising and falling of the ocean, caused by the gravitational attraction of the Sun and Moon.

Titans the giants born of Uranus and Gaia, who ruled Earth until they were overthrown by Cronus's children, the new gods.

trans-Neptunian objects an area of the solar system beyond Neptune that contains millions of icy, cometlike objects. They are also called Kuiper Belt objects.

underworld the place where souls went after death, also known as Hades.

universe the entire celestial world.

zodiac an imaginary circle in the sky, divided into the 12 constellations where the Sun, Moon, and planets appear to travel. The constellations, or signs, of the zodiac are Aries, Taurus, Gemini, Cancer, Leo, Virgo, Libra, Scorpio, Sagittarius, Capricorn, Aquarius, and Pisces.

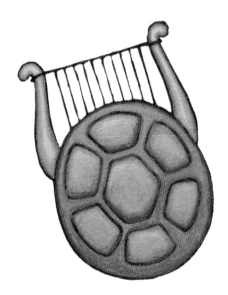

About the Author/Illustrator

Joan Marie Galat lives near Edmonton, Alberta, where she works as a writer on various websites. Joan has contributed to a number of publications on a freelance basis, as well as writing for corporate clients. Her projects have encompassed speech writing, radio scripts, and exhibit text, as well as multimedia and animation projects. Joan's first book was *Dot to Dot in the Sky: Stories in the Stars*. She was formerly published under the name Joan Hinz.

Joan has been a frequent presenter at schools. She enjoys giving writing workshops, as well as sharing her knowledge of the night sky with students of all ages. Her website at www.joangalat.com contains additional author information, astronomy links, and fun for kids.

Lorna Bennett was born in Edmonton, Alberta. She studied Fine Arts in college and university, and has been working in design, illustration and fine art ever since. She enjoys working in a variety of mediums, especially ink, watercolor, pastel and oil paints. When Lorna is not busy working on children's picture books, novel covers, multimedia projects and teaching drawing in elementary schools, she loves to mountain bike, read, cook, watch great movies, and plan where she would like to travel to next.